Strategic Planning for Elected Officials: Setting Priorities

Lydian Altman, Margaret F. Henderson,
and Vaughn Mamlin Upshaw

UNC
SCHOOL OF
GOVERNMENT

The School of Government at the University of North Carolina at Chapel Hill works to improve the lives of North Carolinians by engaging in practical scholarship that helps public officials and citizens understand and improve state and local government. Established in 1931 as the Institute of Government, the School provides educational, advisory, and research services for state and local governments. The School of Government is also home to a nationally ranked Master of Public Administration program, the North Carolina Judicial College, and specialized centers focused on community and economic development, information technology, and environmental finance.

As the largest university-based local government training, advisory, and research organization in the United States, the School of Government offers up to 200 courses, webinars, and specialized conferences for more than 12,000 public officials each year. In addition, faculty members annually publish approximately 50 books, manuals, reports, articles, bulletins, and other print and online content related to state and local government. The School also produces the *Daily Bulletin Online* each day the General Assembly is in session, reporting on activities for members of the legislature and others who need to follow the course of legislation.

Operating support for the School of Government's programs and activities comes from many sources, including state appropriations, local government membership dues, private contributions, publication sales, course fees, and service contracts.

Visit sog.unc.edu or call 919.966.5381 for more information on the School's courses, publications, programs, and services.

Printed in the United States of America

21 20 19 18 17 1 2 3 4 5

ISBN 978-1-56011-877-0

♾ This publication is printed on permanent, acid-free paper in compliance with the North Carolina General Statutes.

♲ Printed on recycled paper

About the Series

Local Government Board Builders offers local elected leaders practical advice on how to effectively lead and govern. Each of the booklets in this series provides a topic overview, and many offer specific tips on effective practice, worksheets, and reflection questions to help local elected leaders improve their work. The series focuses on common activities for local governing boards, such as selecting and appointing committees and advisory boards, planning for the future, making better decisions, improving board accountability, and effectively engaging stakeholders in public decisions.

Vaughn Mamlin Upshaw, lecturer in public administration and government at the UNC School of Government, is the series editor.

Other Books in This Series

Leading Your Governing Board: A Guide for Mayors and County Board Chairs,
Vaughn Mamlin Upshaw, 2009

A Model Code of Ethics for North Carolina Local Elected Officials, A. Fleming Bell, II, 2010

Creating and Maintaining Effective Local Government Citizen Advisory Committees,
Vaughn Mamlin Upshaw, 2010

Working with Nonprofit Organizations, Margaret Henderson, Lydian Altman,
Suzanne Julian, Gordon P. Whitaker, and Eileen R. Youens, 2010

Public Outreach and Participation, John B. Stephens, Ricardo S. Morse, and
Kelley T. O'Brien, 2011

Local Government Revenue Sources in North Carolina, Kara A. Millonzi, 2011

Getting the Right Fit: The Governing Board's Role in Hiring a Manager,
Vaughn Mamlin Upshaw, John A. Rible IV, and Carl W. Stenberg, 2011

The Property Tax in North Carolina, Christopher B. McLaughlin, 2012

Local Government Budgeting: A Guide for North Carolina Elected Officials, Julie M. Brenman with Gregory S. Allison, 2013

Handbook for North Carolina Mayors and Council Members, David M. Lawrence, 2013

How Are We Doing? Evaluating Manager and Board Performance, Vaughn Mamlin Upshaw, 2014

Wicked Problems: What Can Local Governments Do? Eric M. Reese and Maureen M. Berner, 2014

Suggested Rules of Procedure for the Board of County Commissioners, Joseph S. Ferrell, Third Edition, 2002

Suggested Rules of Procedure for Small Local Government Boards, A. Fleming Bell, II, Second Edition, 1998

Suggested Rules of Procedure for a City Council, A. Fleming Bell, II, Third Edition, 2000

Acknowledgments

This publication is dedicated to retired School of Government faculty member Gordon Whitaker, whose leadership and insights helped shape our views on strategic thinking.

We also want to acknowledge Sarah Alongi Forbes, a 2014 graduate of the School of Government Master of Public Administration program whose organizational and analytical skills improved our work on this project.

Lydian Altman
Margaret F. Henderson
Vaughn Mamlin Upshaw

Chapel Hill
December 2016

Contents

Why Plan? 1

- Plans Provide a Path to Success 2
- Plans Save Time 2
- Plans Anchor Priorities 2
- Plans Reduce Conflict 3
- Plans Save Money 3
- Plans Increase Efficiency 3
- Plans Offer Stability 3

What Role Does the Elected Official Play in Strategic Planning? 5

Getting Ready 9

How to Approach Strategic Planning 15

- Strategic Public Leadership 15

Phase One—*Envision*: Where Do We Want to Be? 21

- Key Process—Context: Where Have We Been, and Where Are We Now? 24
- Key Process—Goals and Objectives: What Will We Do? 28

Phase Two—*Enact*: How Will We Get Where We Want to Go? 33

- Key Process—Develop Action Plans: How Can We Make Each Goal Happen? 34
- Key Process—Allocate Resources: What Is Needed to Achieve Our Goals? 38

Phase Three—*Evaluate*: Are We Making Progress? How Successful Are We? 41

- Key Process—Monitoring and Managing Performance: How Are We Doing? 42
- Key Process—Evaluate Results: Are We There Yet? 42

Reality Checks: Tailoring the Process to Fit Your Needs 47

- How Big Do We Want This Process to Be? 47
- How Much Citizen Engagement Is Enough? 48
- Are We Really Ready? 49

Appendix: The Basic Elements of a Strategic Plan 51

Why Plan?

When our coauthor Vaughn Upshaw was a teenager, her father told her, "A wise person dreams at night and works during the day." We think it was good advice forty years ago and remains good advice today.

The term *strategic planning* describes a process through which people first agree on a desired future and then organize their resources and efforts toward meeting those long-term goals. A strategic plan is essentially a dream for your organization. It offers everyone a picture of what you want to accomplish and a vision to work toward. Without a clear vision of what we want to create, it's hard to stay focused on priorities. When nothing is a priority, everything is.

What are your dreams for your community? How do these dreams match the priorities for your local government? Do others share your dreams? How do you know if you and others are working toward the same goals?

If you aren't sure your dreams are the same, or if you find people are focusing on too many small details,[1] consider setting aside the time and resources to create a strategic plan. There are many ways to design strategic plans,[2] and it is beneficial to select a process designed for your situation. At a minimum, a good plan will set forth a long-term vision of what people want their community to look like and identify a handful of broad goals (3 to 5) that will move the community toward that vision.

Strategic planning can help turn your dreams into reality. Developing a long-term plan and getting buy-in may seem like a waste of time, but the failure to plan usually results in wasted effort and resources. Our experience as trainers and facilitators has shown us that

---

1. See Peg Carlson, "If You Don't Want Your Board to Get 'Into the Weeds' . . . Stop Holding Your Retreats in a Vacant Lot," http://leadership.sog.unc.edu/if-you-dont-want-your-board-to-get-into-the-weeds-stop-holding-your-retreats-in-a-vacant-lot. Also see Vaughn Upshaw, "Dreaming Works," http://leadership.sog.unc.edu/dreaming-works.

2. See the Strategic Public Leadership microsite on the UNC School of Government website, www.sog.unc.edu/resources/microsites/strategic-public-leadership#!#https:%2F%2Fwww.sog.unc.edu%2Fresources%2Fmicrosites%2Fstrategic-public-leadership.

strategic planning can be quite beneficial to organizations and communities. This book is our way of offering those potential benefits to others.

Plans Provide a Path to Success

Building on what was done before and setting forth goals that keep a major project moving forward are how organizations produce results. Without a plan, we are more likely to pursue small goals that satisfy individual interests rather than tackle the big issues extending beyond any individual's term in office.

Plans Save Time

It takes less effort to align people and resources around clear and common goals than it does to reorganize every year in response to changing priorities. Without shared goals, management is less efficient because attention and resources are divided and the public is unsure if leaders care about the community's "real" priorities.

Plans Anchor Priorities

A candidate's short term promises often conflict with a governing board's long-term goals. When elected and appointed officials agree on strategic priorities for a community, success is much easier to achieve. Few public issues are resolved in a single term of office. All elected officials benefit when they can point to how they are making progress on strategic issues for the community.

Plans Reduce Conflict

When people agree on big goals, they do not bicker as much over smaller decisions about what to do. Well-crafted, big-picture goals provide community and local government leaders with a framework that encourages buy-in as well as agreement on how to allocate resources and take action.

Plans Save Money

Clear goals help focus limited resources on agreed upon priorities. Without clear goals, resources may be insufficient to meet critical needs or, worse, used in ways that undermine the achievement of important objectives.

Plans Increase Efficiency

When people at every level, from board members to frontline staff, know where they want to go and what they want to achieve, they focus more on tasks and actions that matter.

Plans Offer Stability

Elected and appointed leaders move, retire, and shift roles in local governments. Changes in leadership can result in a revolving door of priorities. Well-developed long-term goals provide a foundation on which new leaders can be oriented, budgets can be organized, and outcomes can be measured.

What Role Does the Elected Official Play in Strategic Planning?

A strategic plan provides a focus to guide decisions and actions related to resource allocation, policy development, accountability, and transparency. It can be particularly valuable to public leaders who want to be forward-thinking and build consensus on the direction and intent of long-term initiatives to improve their communities.

The decision to engage in strategic planning should originate with the elected officials since they are responsible for the long-term health and well-being of their community. Investments in public infrastructure or policies about land use are core to how a community gets shaped or reshaped over time, and these decisions are fundamental to the job of an elected official. If governing boards and senior management do not initiate and support the planning process, there is no reason to invest resources in the work. Only when the elected officials and senior managers are committed to strategic planning will the efforts be sustained over time.

Although others may be invited to participate in the process, the *elected governing board and senior management are responsible for setting the direction and holding each other and the organization accountable* for making progress toward achieving agreed upon goals. Others play an important role too. Everyone in the organization—department heads to frontline workers—should inform leaders about trends and priorities and engage in work that supports goals identified during the planning process.

Effective leaders take time to understand the context of what is happening locally, regionally, nationally, and globally and to ask how these changes will impact their communities over time. There is much we do not know about the future, but some facts we know to be true: the world around us is changing. It will not remain static or return to the way it once was. Information about a community's past patterns and present context is available; using it to shape the future requires leadership.

Using a comprehensive strategic planning process enables leaders to thoughtfully engage others and exercise financial stewardship as they work to improve the quality of community life over time. Most communities face issues that are difficult to identify, are persistent, and that affect various sectors of the population. These wicked problems cannot be solved by one sector, a single organization, or leader working on their own. It takes the focus and commitment of many in and out of local government to progress.

When times are tough, community leaders must act with intention in order to change the trajectory. Unlike a private sector organization that can pick up and move if the going gets rough, a city or county stays put. Disengaging, denying the realities, or ignoring trends is not an option for local governments. Leaders can make the difference by stepping up.

Creating a different future requires leaders to think and behave differently. The old saying that "insanity is doing the same thing over and over again and expecting a different result" may mean that an infusion of creativity and thinking outside the box is required as leaders work to create a future that is quite different from what existed in the past. *The purpose of this publication is to describe a process that public leaders can use to move communities forward toward intentional goals.*

Strategic public leadership offers an opportunity for local governments to demonstrate congruency between their core activities or functions and their agreed upon strategies. Successfully implementing the process outlined here will require additional administrative and facilitative tools and techniques that are beyond the scope of this publication. It is essential, however, that elected and appointed leaders understand and commit to a shared planning process that focuses on and aligns resources with stated goals and uses communication and accountability systems to ensure that efforts are progressing and producing intended outcomes.

School of Government Recommended Best Practices for Conducting Successful Strategic Plans

- We advise significant, meaningful *engagement* by those in the organization and others who are clearly affected by the goals and anticipated changes.
- We endorse *facilitative leadership* that promotes the leader as facilitator and convener rather than the developer and the teller.
- We encourage *shared learning*—a co-equal approach to framing the questions to help the organization improve, and to apply to broader public administration interests.
- We suggest *flexibility* in responding to emerging needs or unexpected opportunities.
- We discuss and demonstrate *accountability and transparency* and expect the client to be committed to practicing the same.

The following guidelines can help leaders engage in a successful planning process:

- *Imagine your community's best future.* Board members and senior managers use a structured process to focus on the future of their community. They put aside business-as-usual agendas to generate a compelling image of the future that will guide critical short- and long-term decision-making.
- *Adopt a learning mindset.* Participants have to be willing to learn from—then put aside—issues of the past or the present and think about what they want to do differently going forward.
- *Agree upon and act on shared goals.* Once leaders agree on a preferred image of the future, professionals, experts, and partners can be brought in to offer technical assistance, determine necessary resources, and develop action plans.
- *Hold yourselves and others accountable.* Once a strategic plan is adopted, leaders throughout the organization must hold themselves accountable to achieve defined goals. The board and senior managers do this by ensuring that they invest public resources, make timely decisions, and provide services that are consistent with and make progress toward accomplishing their vision for the community.

Level of Involvement: Telling, Selling, Testing, Consulting, Co-creating

Low	**Telling** I tell you what you need to know about my plan.	**"We've got to do this. It's our vision/plan. You be excited about it."** Elected body imposes vision. Stakeholders don't get a voice.
	Selling I tell you about my plan and convince you to go along with it.	**"We have the best answer. Let's see if we can get *you* to buy in."** Elected body develops vision. Enroll stakeholders in the vision.
	Testing I'm thinking about doing it this way. What do you think?	**"What excites *you* about this work? What doesn't?"** Gauge acceptance, support, and relevance of the elected body's view point. If there is not sufficient community support, officials go back to the drawing board. Success depends on stakeholders' willingness to be truthful and realistic.*
High	**Consulting** What do you think we should do, given these criteria and resources?	**"What vision/plan do *other stakeholders* recommend that we adopt?"** Engage stakeholders in designing the vision and considering the ramifications of various choices;* elected body plays role of judge in accepting/ignoring what stakeholders say. Officials determine the content of the vision and decide how to begin moving in that direction.

*Do various stakeholders know enough about the roles and responsibilities of local government to be able to make these judgments or understand the ramifications of decisions? If not, stakeholders will have to be educated in using this approach.

Adapted from Peter M. Senge, Art Kleiner, Charlotte Roberts, Richard B. Ross, and Bryan J. Smith, *The Fifth Discipline Fieldbook: Strategies and Tools for Building a Learning Organization* (New York: Doubleday, 1994). For more guidance in managing citizen engagement, see Upshaw, *Creating and Maintaining Effective Local Government Citizen Advisory Committees.*

Getting Ready

As the governing board and senior management team begin to consider undertaking a strategic planning effort, the following questions will help them determine its potential value to the local community.

Why and how do we want to engage in a strategic leadership process? Many different motivations and expectations may be held by the board and senior managers. Seeing and hearing their different purposes can help leaders identify common interests. It is unlikely that any local government will have the time or resources to support every purpose. Clarifying why strategic planning benefits your community and/or organization and determining how you want to approach the process are necessary prerequisites to moving forward.

How far into the future do we want to plan? How might our plan accommodate short- and long-term goals? Some organizations may choose to integrate strategic planning into annual work plans—for example, following an annual planning retreat with elected officials the town manager allocates resources toward meeting the strategic priorities set at the retreat and then, throughout the year, updates the governing board as to the progress being made toward reaching those goals. Other communities might focus their strategic process on a particular project. Still others could decide to cast a long-range vision of ten to fifteen years and then create a near-term (two to three years) plan for achieving that vision.

How broadly does our vision reach? Are we interested in dreaming about the community's future, its organizations, or both? Keep in mind, if a plan focuses on a singular challenge, such as financing and building a new facility, then limiting participants primarily to people in your local government makes sense. In contrast, particularly complex or strategic issues, such as workforce preparedness, will require broader participation if a strategic goal is to be realized.

How can we design a process that includes input and buy-in from all those needed to accomplish it? Local leaders are usually interested in incorporating some sort of community or stakeholder input into their strategic planning process but are unclear on the extent of involvement they desire and what will be done.

Elements of Strategic Planning and Community Visioning

This chart represents some boundaries for making decisions regarding strategic planning. Most planning efforts incorporate elements from both columns.

	Strategic Planning	Community Visioning
Focus	❑ Organization	❑ Community
Purpose	❑ What priorities do we have as we seek to fulfill our mission?	❑ What kind of community do we want to be?
Participants	❑ Governing board, management, and employees	❑ Broad spectrum of community stakeholders
Expected Outcomes	❑ Future trends and impacts for organizational/community consideration and response identified ❑ Desired changes or conditions named and prioritized (goals and strategies) ❑ SMART objectives developed (*Specific, Measurable, Aggressive yet Attainable, Realistic, and Time-bound*) ❑ Responsibility for actions and tasks identified ❑ Preliminary benchmarks and timelines for implementing strategies set	
Process	❑ Initial exploration and data gathering SWOC analysis (*Strengths, Weaknesses, Opportunities, Challenges*) ❑ Assess the specific area of focus* ❑ Set or affirm vision, mission, goals, and objectives ❑ Choose objectives that will demonstrate change ❑ Identify, evaluate, and prioritize projects ❑ Develop detailed and specific plans of action, including measures of performance ❑ Implement plans and allocate resources ❑ Monitor and evaluate outcomes ❑ Retool and readjust periodically	In addition to items listed in left column: ❑ Document anecdotal stories ❑ Mobilize local and non-local resources ❑ Expand and enrich the capacity of the non-governmental sector ❑ Engage broad representation that reflects the community

(*continued*)

	Strategic Planning	Community Visioning
Considerations	❑ Leads to more of the same or incremental change ❑ May overlook organization's role in addressing broader priorities and achieving larger community goals ❑ Plan potential may not be fully realized; links to other management areas not adequately clear or utilized (e.g., allocating resources, managing progress, or evaluating results)	❑ Requires substantive understanding of the community ❑ Calls for skills in using tools for community-wide strategic thinking and analysis ❑ Can be unwieldy, leading to too many goals and diffuse authority ❑ Potential reactions by those providing input if that input isn't seen as being useful to organizers or included, reflected in final plan
Time Frame	❑ Varies, but usually completed in 3 to 6 months	❑ Varies, but usually completed in 12 to 18 months
Accountability for Process and Outcomes	❑ Governing board, senior management, and employees	❑ Community organizations, businesses, local government, educational institutions, other stakeholders in the community vision

*The plan may be broad or center on specific subjects, such as economic development, land use, or infrastructure needs. Similarly, an organization's plan can be focused inward (to organizational reactions), outward, or both.

No matter how the planning process is designed, the community should assess whether it has the people, commitment, resources, and time to implement it successfully.

For more information, contact Lydian Altman, director, Strategic Public Leadership Initiative, at 919.962.0103 or lydian@sog.unc.edu.

The scope of the vision that leaders envisage will influence the design of your planning process. An all-encompassing community vision is best developed by involving a wide range of community stakeholders (example: representatives of public and private sector organizations as well as people who live, work, worship, shop, and play in the community). Alternatively, a vision to address a single critical issue, such as workforce preparedness, will involve a more narrow set of participants (example: employers, educational institutions, community development agencies).

What will be different as a result of our having developed a strategic plan? In any plan, you expect to find a series of goals or statements about the conditions you want to be different, the changes you believe are necessary to reach that new and different state, and a series of strategies—or a collection of actions and tasks—that will move you toward this new situation or desired state. How a community defines those specifics will vary.

Specific actions and outcomes aside, the process of undertaking the strategic planning effort will position participants in ways that can shape the future. If you haven't been planning, you can't start to work with any focus, clarity of purpose, or knowledge about how others could possibly influence the work in a direction you favor. Moreover, it is simply a plan for what has not yet happened, so conditions are likely to change.

Plans will undoubtedly be tweaked and changed over time to respond to unexpected events, so the planning process is at least as important as the plan itself. Or as President Dwight D. Eisenhower put it in a November 1957 speech before the National Defense Executive Reserve Conference, "That is the reason it is so important to plan, to keep yourselves steeped in the character of the problem that you may one day be called upon to solve—or to help to solve."

How do we intend to use our plan? Many organizations consider the plan to be done once it has been developed and adopted by the elected body. If this is the case, the plan will fall short of its full potential and could end up as a credenza filler rather than a living document.

A strategic plan is more likely to be successful when it is combined with other uses and purposes within an organization. Engaging and enabling multiple aspects of the organization creates the broader multi-pronged ability to move the organization or community toward the desired future.

Making the decision about how you might use your strategic plan before you begin planning could help you think more broadly and might influence the processes used throughout its development. The following list describes the various ways that successful boards, organizations, and communities combine strategic planning with other organizational practices. This can be accomplished either intentionally—for example, by co-developing the work—or more organically.

- *Benchmarking*: Choose key measurements to track as indicators of achievement toward a desired goal. An example would be to benchmark the turnaround times when public vehicles become inoperable, come in for repair, and are then returned to working order. Doing so can help assess the impact of system improvements to maintenance and repair services.
- *Performance Evaluation*: Assign action steps to specific staff to ensure and track the progress of implementation.
- *Budgeting/Resource Allocation*: Make decisions to invest resources in such a way to further the priority goals.
- *Internal and External Communication*: Use the format of the plan as a tool for reporting progress to others.
- *Citizen Engagement and Education*: Create opportunities for citizens to hear information and provide input to either the creation or implementation of the plan.
- *Employee Orientation*: Use the plan to recruit and orient new employees by explaining what the organization is working toward as well as how each person is expected to contribute to making progress through specific goals and action steps.
- *Disciplined Attention*: The plan can help focus the governing board's attention on community and organizational priorities.

How will we proceed to conduct the work? You've decided on the breadth and scope of your plan, defined who you want to involve in your planning effort and how, and considered how your plan can be useful to your organization or community. You're ready! Now what? Who is going to conduct and/or direct the work? Do you have the capacity within your organization to undertake the effort? Are there reasons why engaging an external consultant or facilitator to guide your process makes sense? What resources could you offer to leverage the contributions of an outside consultant?

Ideally the choice of whether to use a consultant or facilitator should happen before too much discussion about your strategic planning objectives takes place. A facilitator can provide valuable guidance and assistance to the planning group as you design the work, assess your needs, and make other planning decisions.

Beyond offering technical skills or knowledge, two of the most often cited reasons to use a consultant or facilitator is to help keep the group focused and to ensure that all participants participate fully in the discussion. Yet securing a trained and neutral facilitator with whom the entire group is comfortable will take time, effort, and money. You may choose to look internally for someone with the skills you desire or for volunteers within your community who could help. Such resources include area council of governments, community colleges, state agencies, or cooperative extension offices. More information about finding the right facilitation fit for strategic planning or shorter term retreats can be found on the Elected Board Retreats microsite on the School of Government's website.[3]

---

3. See www.sog.unc.edu/resources/microsites/elected-board-retreats/finding-right-facilitation-fit.

How to Approach Strategic Planning

Organizations and communities are generally motivated to engage in strategic planning because they agree on a destination and want a common roadmap on how to get there. Many different approaches and tools are available to groups that want to engage in this process. Typical strategic planning processes focus on developing a plan and establishing priorities for action. The process outlined in this publication goes further than most planning approaches by including guidelines for monitoring and evaluating success.

Strategic Public Leadership

The Strategic Public Leadership (SPL) approach developed by professionals and faculty at the UNC School of Government goes beyond developing a plan. The SPL cycle (see Figure 1) connects work typically associated with the creation of a strategic plan with activities needed to implement and evaluate that work. This guidebook provides an overview of the three-phase SPL cycle and the work that needs to take place at each phase.

The first phase of the process is to *envision* achievable goals informed by data and history. The task of the second phase, *enact*, is to develop action plans and allocate resources. The final phase, *evaluate*, requires leaders to monitor progress and review results. The SPL cycle ties strategic goals to actionable priorities, budget items, and monitoring systems. And, while no model can guarantee success, the SPL cycle offers leaders a framework to

- focus on and remind themselves as well as others about strategic priorities,
- align resources with agreed upon goals, and
- track performance, services, and processes that contribute to desired outcomes.

Using the SPL cycle helps an organization become clear about its challenges and opportunities. Once goals are explored, narrowed, and agreed upon, a strategic plan gives leaders a way to prioritize actions, allocate existing resources, or find new resources in order to progress toward those goals.

Figure 1. Strategic Public Leadership Cycle

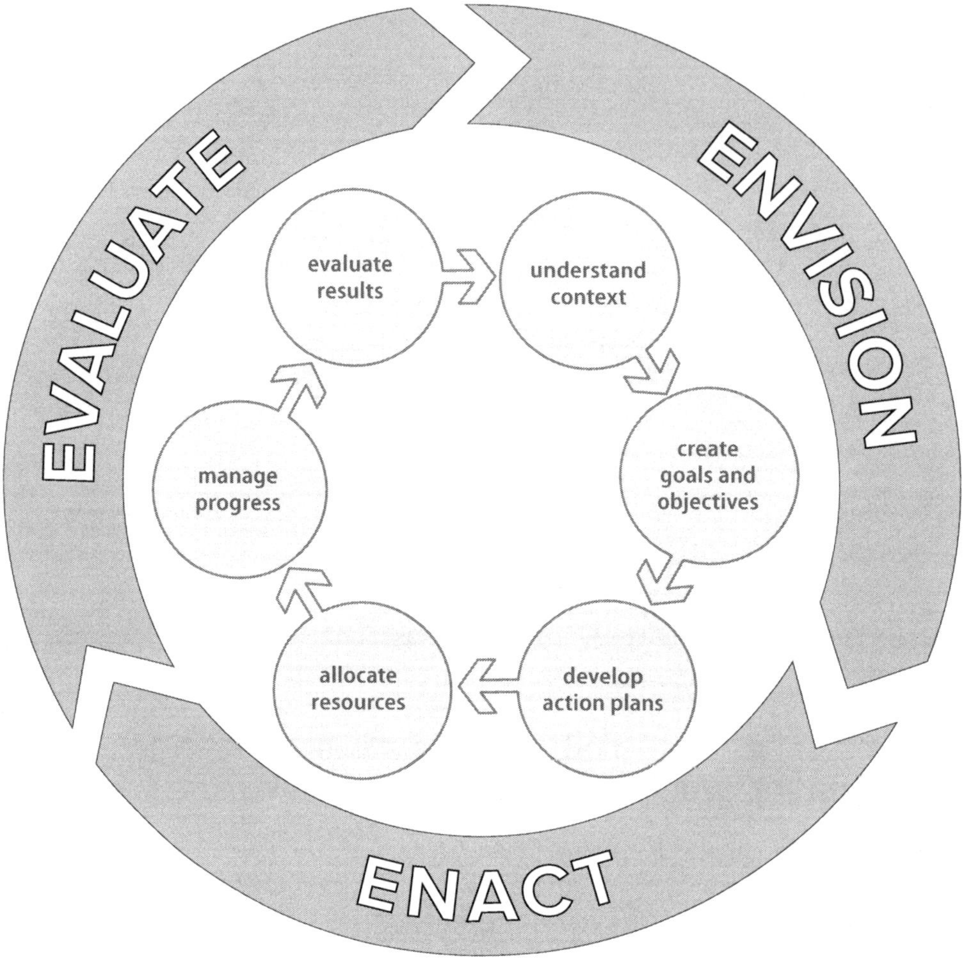

By defining what "success" and "progress" look like, leadership and management can better organize work and establish meaningful ways to determine whether activities are contributing to goals as intended. Others will see how they contribute to success when their organizational activities and programs are tied to strategic goals. Thoughtful and deliberate plans, tied to resources and activities, can help people stay focused even as things change. For example, a good strategic planning process can help orient newcomers to the board and the organization as to where the organization has been and where it wants to go.

Leaders should reach out and ask those who have a role in accomplishing goals to help set them. Participants in the planning and implementation processes need to be given opportunities to share their expertise and insights, to build relationships with each other, and to use that shared experience as a foundation for future action together. Long-term goals often require efforts by multiple people and organizations. If others have a significant responsibility to help meet a strategic goal, then they need to be involved in setting targets, developing action plans, and allocating resources. Planning something for others to do without their direct involvement will inevitably fail.

Before undertaking any strategic planning process, leaders need to be clear about why strategic planning is needed and how the process will be used. Initial discussions about why to engage in strategic planning are likely to be broad and conceptual. As people share their hopes and fears about engaging in the work, however, reasons for engaging in strategic planning will become increasingly clear. Such conversations can, at times, be messy and interests may appear to be contradictory.

At the outset, leaders need to be engaged in clarifying expectations and agreeing on the focus of the strategic planning effort. As soon as a strategic planning process gets under way, a myriad of issues will surface, some of which may not seem relevant to the work. For strategic planning to be meaningful and relevant to all participants, leaders need to simultaneously agree on the general direction and scope of the planning effort while allowing previously unrecognized opportunities and unidentified or unacknowledged problems to be considered and incorporated into the plan, as appropriate, as the process unfolds.

In order to approach strategic planning holistically rather than as a single exercise, leaders need to ask and answer the following questions:

- Why do we want to do strategic (long-term) planning?
- Who are we planning for (organization, community, region, other)?
- Who has a stake in our strategic plan? Whom will our planning affect? Who will affect our long-term success?
- If our process is successful, how will things be different five years from now?
- How much will we commit to our strategic planning effort (staff, money, time, etc.)?

In summary, the SPL cycle differs from traditional strategic planning. Instead of simply creating a planning document, it structures a series of events and processes that

- tie board goals to management actions,
- create tracking systems for monitoring progress, and
- enable the accountability of management and decision-makers.

This cycle produces strategic plans with greater impact by

- emphasizing the *ongoing connections and alignments* between the plan and other parts of the organization,
- adding project *implementation, accountability, and follow-up* to the planning process, and
- translating "big ideas" into measurable goals and action plans with *tracking systems* to ensure that staff and decision-makers are accountable.

The SPL approach to long-term planning described herein outlines what has to be done, when it should be done, and how each phase informs the next. It reflects best practices consistent with thinking-planning-doing-evaluating-learning systems that help leaders, organizations, and communities learn from their successes and mistakes and stay on track for creating a desired future. The "Why Engage in Strategic Planning?" sidebar provides a few questions and answers about the SPL approach, while the case problem "Who Needs to Know" describes how one county government used SPL to make adjustments in how they conduct business during periods of economic recession and transitions in leadership but missed the step of sharing information about the process and its outcomes throughout local government.

Case Problem: Who Needs to Know?

Motivated by a tighter economy, one local government embarked on a long-term SPL process and started by creating a vision for the future and establishing six focus areas around which they would align efforts across departments. The elected officials worked with senior staff to identify core services, and each service was linked to one or more of the six focus areas. In the next budget, the commissioners approved resources to support their priorities, and personnel changes were made as well. The governing board then turned its attention to its dozens of advisory committees—many of which had lost focus, duplicated or contradicted each other, and were affecting the best use of employees' and elected officials' time and effort. The commissioners reduced the overall number and matched the purposes of advisory boards with the county's overall focus areas.

Months later, a School of Government instructor used the county's work as an example of the SPL process in practice, demonstrating how leaders were using the plan to discipline themselves to achieve their desired goals. An employee from the county's budget office just happened to be in the audience and commented, "Oh, now it all makes sense. I didn't understand that was what they were doing."

This example serves as a reminder that an organization benefits when its leaders share information about the process and its outcomes across all layers of the government—up, down, and across; to elected and appointed officials, staff, and volunteers.

Why Engage in Strategic Planning?

What Are the Goals of Strategic Planning?

- To be clear about priorities.
- To allocate resources toward those priorities.
- To manage performance to carry out the funded programs.
- To evaluate performance in terms of objectives.

What Is Strategic Public Leadership?

- A way for elected leaders and public managers to plan for and work toward a desired vision of the future.

Why Use the SPL Process?

SPL produces a *plan* with *legs* that . . .

- provides guidance on where we are going, what we will do to get there, and how we will do the work;
- reflects shared values;
- transforms dreams to into actions;
- aligns resources to achieve goals;
- tracks progress and learns to improve;
- adapts to short-term realities while pursuing long-term goals.

What Must Leaders Do to Carry Out the SPL Process?

SPL is carried out by *leaders* who . . .

- practice what they preach;
- inspire vivid, positive possibilities;
- seek opportunities, seize the initiative;
- engage others inside and outside the organization in their work;
- celebrate accomplishments toward strategic goals.

Phase One—*Envision*: Where Do We Want to Be?

The envisioning phase of the SPL cycle includes two key processes—understanding the context for the plan and creating goals and objectives (see Figure 2). Each of these processes requires leaders and participants to engage in a series of discussions and activities that culminate in a clear vision of the future as well as agreement on the most important ways to organize the work in order to make the vision a reality.

This guidebook presents an overview of envisioning activities, each of which generates a product that goes into the final plan. Table 1 summarizes the activities and products typically used during the envision phase. Each process, activity, and product produced is described in greater detail below.

The first activity in the envisioning phase is to imagine and agree on a shared picture of what participants want their community or organization to look like in the future. This dreaming of the future is necessary for a number of reasons. Having people talk about what their preferred future looks like helps others understand what people care about and what in the current environment is not meeting their expectations or could be improved. Another reason is that dreaming about where they want to go uncovers commonalities among participants and begins to create networks for change. A vision statement succinctly

Figure 2. Where Do We Want to Be?

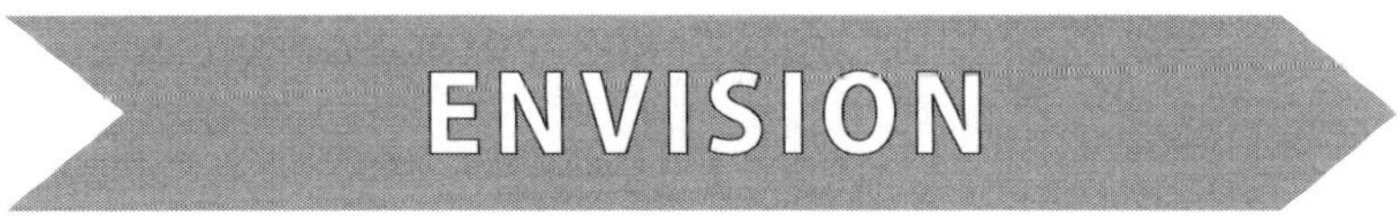

- **Understand context**
- **Create goals and objectives**

Table 1. Key Processes, Activities, and Products in the SPL Cycle's *Envision* Phase

***Envision*: Where Do We Want to Be?**

Key Process	Activities	Products
Understand context	• Imagining the future • How we work • Agree on important words • Review history and trends • Organizational readiness	• Vision statement • Mission and values • Glossary • Impact time line • SOAR
Create goals and objectives	• Lumping and splitting • Goal setting	• Labeled "buckets" • Strategic goals

embodies the common aspirations for the organization or community. Participants are energized by trying to envision where the organization and/or community will be in the next five, ten, or twenty years, and doing so provides a constant reminder of why this process matters—especially when things, as they inevitably do, get harder.

Two additional activities and products coincide with the creation of the Vision statement—development and/or refinement of the organization's mission and values (see Table 2). Taken together, the Vision, Mission, and Values statements provide guideposts that can be used to get people back on track whenever the conversation or a situation becomes cluttered, frustrating, or confusing.

- The Vision statement is aspirational, reflecting a shared sense of *where* the community will be in the future.
  - *XX years from now, our community will be* ________________________.
- The Mission statement describes *what* your organization does that contributes to the vision.
  - *Our organization actively creates that desired future by* ____________.
- The Values statement describes *how* people carry out their work.
  - *In accomplishing our work, we will* ____________________________.

Start by asking people to individually reflect and make notes on these statements. As individuals compare their mission, vision, and value statements they may discover that

Table 2. Development and/or Refinement of an Organization's Mission and Values

	Activity: Questions for Discussion	Products
Where Do We Want to Go?	1. Why does our organization or community need to exist? What is our reason for being? 2. If our organization or community were the best it could be, what would it look like? 3. How would you describe your organization or community's ideal future in a few words or short phrase?	*Define the Vision.* A vision is the "Big Picture" statement of what your community wants to be. It describes what your community will look like when the mission is accomplished. It is brief, compelling and gives purpose and direction to the organization or community.
	4. What services do we provide to what people, and at what quality and cost? 5. How does our mission relate to our vision? 6. What limits does our mission set for us in accomplishing our vision?	*Define the Mission.* The statement should offer a distinctive reason for the organization to exist and describe its core purpose, be memorable, results-oriented, and actionable.
	7. How can we demonstrate our commitment to the mission and vision? 8. What values guide us every day and in every aspect of our work?	*Define the Values.* Values are the core principles that define the organization's leadership and management style and that guide personal and agency behavior.

equally important interests compete directly—"keep the tax rate the same" versus "provide high-quality education for our children," for example—and discussions can easily become frustrating. The content of the Vision, Mission, or Values statements should articulate the relative emphasis to be placed on existing or future generations, security or risk-taking, independence or collaboration. Using the Vision, Mission, and Value statements to define the intent of this planning process will put competing ideas to the test.

If the group repeatedly gets hung up on a particular word or phrase, that is an indication that the "right" words have not been put on the page or that the most important ideas have yet to be identified and articulated. As such, the group may want to have available draft statements that use similar, but different, words so that they can try them out and assess whether any adjustments are necessary to more accurately capture the interests of the group. Formal approval of the statements can wait until the end stage of the planning process.

Just as it is important to get the words right in your guiding documents, it is useful to identify and define commonly used words and terms and start developing a glossary. For participants to agree on specific definitions of key words, phrases, and acronyms, they need to be sure that they are talking about the same things. People can mean quite different things when using the same words, especially if the words are abstract. Asking each other for clarification and agreeing on what important words mean can help ensure that people stay on the same track as they go through the SPL process.

Key Process—Context: Where Have We Been, and Where Are We Now?

As we have shown, the *envision* phase encourages participants to be aspirational and idealistic about the future. But before a group jumps directly into deciding how to achieve such an exciting new vision, people need to first reflect on how they got to where they are now and what this history and experience tell them about the future (Figure 3).

A useful way to have people put their dreams into context is to create an organizational or community time line that includes major historical milestones and events as well as information about the impact of these events on the organization or community. Such time lines can be simple or complex, depending on how the organization wants to use them. At a minimum, a time line should include major events that have had a significant effect on the community over the past 100 years, such as,

- key events occurring in the community (major disasters, significant economic change, leadership shift),
- key events occurring in the state (policy changes, investments, demographic movements), and
- key events occurring at the national/global level (wars, climate change, economic policies, investments in infrastructure).

Looking at the time line, participants should ask themselves

- Who were community leaders during this time, and how did they respond to the events that affected them? Did our leaders boldly face the challenges, or did they pull back?
- When did our organization or community respond successfully to the challenges/opportunities in the environment? When were we less successful?
- As we think about the future we want to create, what can we learn from our past and present about how to be successful? What mistakes do we want to make sure we don't repeat?

Figure 3. Envisioning Where We've Been

Where have we been?

- What have we done well over time?
- What mistakes have we made and how have we responded to them?
- What historical events help us understand how we got to where we are now?
- What can history teach us going forward?

Looking at the drafted Vision, Mission, and Values statements, participants should ask themselves

- How does our vision for the future build on what we've done before?
- How does our mission need to change but also remain the same in order to sustain our good work and avoid mistakes we've made in the past?
- What do we want to remember about our past as we do our work going forward?

To understand our current situation, we have to understand where we have been and how that shaped where we are now (Figure 4). If members of a group hold different understandings of history, discussions about the current situation or the future are likely to be disjointed and frustrating. One person might understand how personal, legal, or financial limitations affected a particular event or issue, for example, while a person without

Figure 4. Where Are We Now?

- **What data is important for your community to focus on?**
- **What's happening in your environment?**
- **Who else influences what's happening in your community?**

that information might conclude that the event or issue was the result of entirely different forces, personalities, or political realities.

Participants move from the present to a more ideal future first by building a factual and shared understanding of the current situation. At the same time, the group needs to guard against engaging in defeatist thinking and becoming stuck in "what is." History and current data must inform the conversation about "what we want to become." Avoid letting current challenges or historical failures limit peoples' dreams for the future. Reframe mistakes as lessons to be used to avoid similar challenges in the future. So, for example, if a developer has left the community with a large, unfinished housing project, the question on the table becomes, "How can we make sure that, going forward, the town only enters into contracts that will hold it harmless?" That a community has always been X does not mean it can never become Y. For an X community to turn into a Y community, people will need to be both open to change and willing to create a unique path going forward.

It also is necessary to be aware that an organization or community might be strongly affected by current or emerging trends and events outside its control. In a complex and intertwined world, it makes less and less sense to think that any one organization or community can work in isolation or independently to solve complicated, hard-to-address,

Discussion: Uncovering and Understanding the Context

Where Have We Been?	1. What have we done well over time? 2. What have been our failures in the past, and how have we responded to them? 3. What historical trends help us understand where we have been and where we are going?	• Consider trends, patterns, history. • Review the data. • Come to a collective agreement about the key points of learning.
Where Are We Now?	1. What do you see that is currently happening or emerging that presents opportunities for the community? 2. As your community progresses in the next 15 years, what specific results are likely to be realized? 3. How can government contribute to the results you want to achieve? 4. Who else needs to be involved to make progress in this area?	• Conduct a situational analysis or environmental scan. • Implement strategies to gain community input, such as through interviews, surveys, forums, or focus groups.

persistent issues, what often are referred to as wicked problems.[4] Therefore, it is important to scan the data and environment for factors that originate elsewhere but have a local impact. Obvious examples include changing legislation, international treaties or conflicts, or even just evolving social expectations. To be successful in strategic leadership, the leaders must engage in expansive thinking about external factors that might affect local dynamics.

Armed with a sense of where the organization and community have come from and where things are today, the leaders are ready to do an analysis to determine the group's readiness to act. One way to explore and understand the organization or community's preparation to act is to conduct a SOAR (Strengths, Opportunities, Aspirations, Results) analysis. This approach is similar to a SWOT (Strengths, Weaknesses, Opportunities, Threats) analysis used in traditional planning processes. The advantage of using a SOAR analysis is that it offers a positive framework for assessing what the organization or community can do and wants to achieve without introducing blame, excuses, or us/them defensiveness (Figure 5).

Once items are generated for each quadrant of the SOAR analysis, the group's task is to infuse that information with meaning. This discussion is geared toward identifying the strategic priorities and goals to be taken up in the subsequent step. Accordingly, the group should reflect on the SOAR analysis by asking such questions as

- How do our strengths position us to be successful moving forward?
- What opportunities have we overlooked or undervalued?
- How do our aspirations support or compete with each other?
- How do the results we desire support or compete with each other?
- Who else needs to be involved to make progress toward taking advantage of the opportunities or achieving any of the desired results?

One challenge of the *envision* phase of the cycle is that people are required to work at the conceptual level. Discussing history and current data necessarily requires a consideration of details. Generally it is easier for people to understand details about who did what to whom and when. This ease often leads groups to become engrossed in a conversation about what kind of flooring to put in the library while ignoring the larger challenge of figuring out how local libraries are to operate in the digital age. When discussions get specific (who did what, when, where, and why), leaders need to remind participants that this phase is

---

4. See Eric M. Reese and Maureen Berner, *Wicked Problems: What Can Local Governments Do?* UNC School of Government (SOG) Local Government Board Builders series (Chapel Hill: SOG, 2014), https://www.sog.unc.edu/publications/books/wicked-problems-what-can-local-governments-do.

Figure 5. Framework for a SOAR Analysis

What are our Strengths?	What are our Opportunities?
What are our Aspirations?	**What Results do we want to see?**

intended to generate big themes that affect the future, not get into the weeds, and redirect the conversation back to the conceptual level.

Key Process—Goals and Objectives: What Will We Do?

At this point, the group has several techniques available to them to review and organize what has been learned about the community or organization's history, current trends, and vision for the future. But, before moving into goals setting, the group needs to *lump* and *split* what has been generated into "like buckets." Activities such as mind mapping, multi-voting exercises, or affinity diagrams can help as the group attempts to organize information into similar categories (see Figure 6). Whichever tool is used, participants should be clear about what is in and what is out of each grouping. After the group has placed everything into buckets that make sense to them, people need to label each category and briefly state how the category relates to and is important to achieving the group's vision for the future.

Exploring the current context and organizing information into broad categories offer participants an opportunity to be active and engaged as they learn about each other's perspectives. This part of the process should be lively, thoughtful, and fun. If designed and run well, this phase will result in participants feeling quite proud of the collective knowledge

Figure 6. Brainstorming Exercises Using Mind Mapping, Multi-voting, and Affinity Diagrams

What do we need to consider in developing a strategic plan?

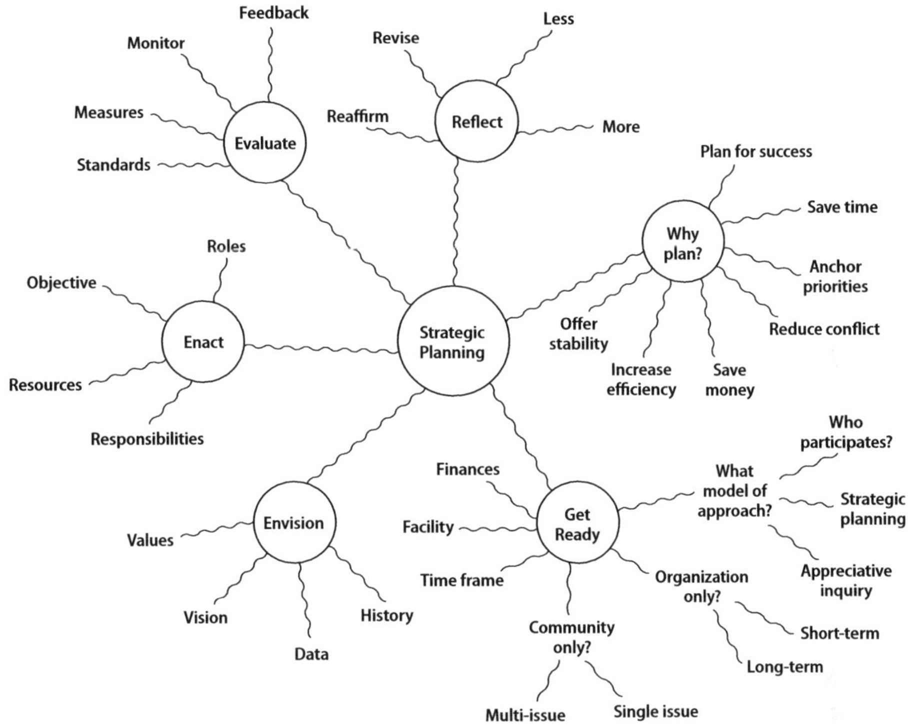

The mind mapping tool is used to visually organize information.

Which is the most important reason for us to have a strategic plan? Why plan?

1. Plan for success	✔	✔	✔				
2. Save time	✔	✔					
3. Anchor priorities	✔	✔	✔	✔	✔		
4. Reduce conflict	✔	✔	✔	✔	✔	✔	✔
5. Save money	✔	✔	✔				
6. Increase efficiency	✔	✔					
7. Offer stability	✔	✔	✔	✔	✔		

Multi-voting is used to shorten a long list of items into a workable number through a series of structured votes.

Figure 6. Brainstorming Exercises Using Mind Mapping, Multi-voting, and Affinity Diagrams (*continued*)

How can strategic planning help reduce organizational conflict?

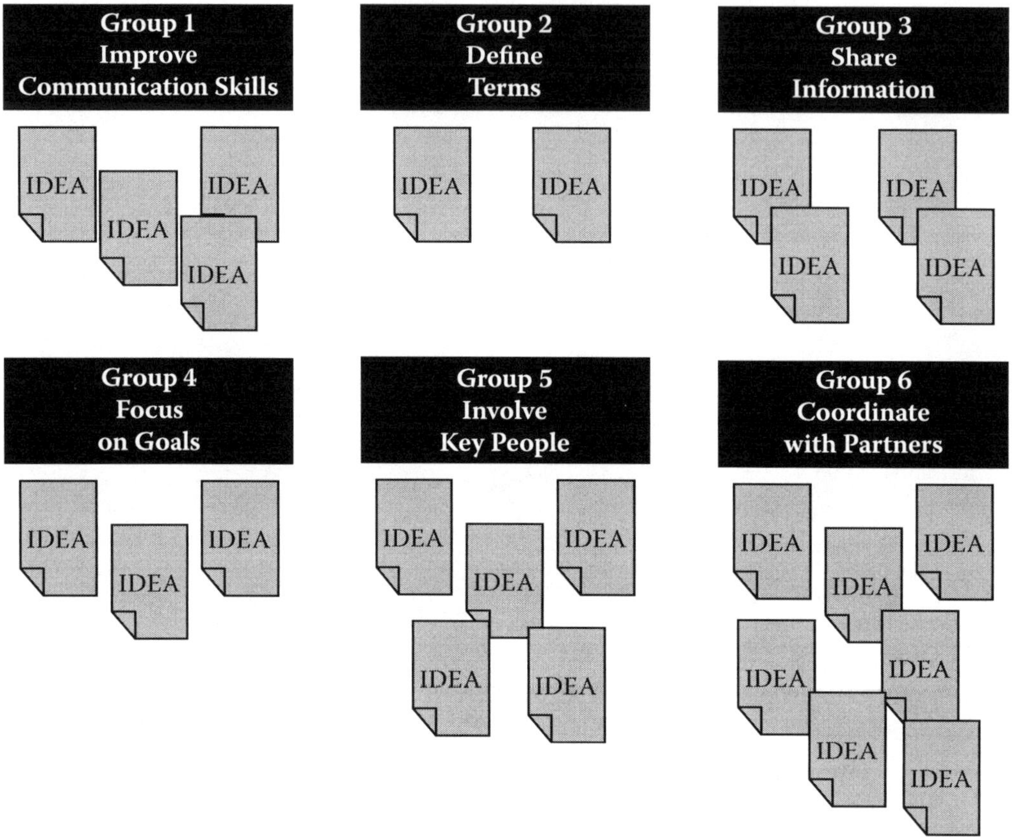

An affinity diagram is used to collect a large amount of data—ideas, opinions, issues—into like groups based on their natural relationships.

and wisdom they have uncovered. The content of the discussion will be shared and brought up in other relevant conversations across the community, and this is a good thing.

At this point in the envisioning phase, people are often eager to "get to work" on the big issues affecting their organization and community, now that they see them more clearly. Leaders, meanwhile, are more focused on developing a common agenda to address these broad priorities, translating them into practicable steps geared toward the organization or community's long-term betterment.

Figure 7. Goal Development

ENVISION

- **What new conditions would you like to see?**
- **What changes would happen if these conditions were occurring?**
- **What important differences would you expect to see from these results?**

Once the group has learned what it can about the current situation, the next step is to build on that knowledge to set specific goals (Figure 7). The purpose of this discussion is to come to agreement on the most compelling changes the organization or community needs to make in moving toward the vision. The conversation might start out in general terms and speak to complex challenges in a way that the issues seem impossible to address. If leaders refer participants back to the Vision, Mission, and Values statements, however, specific goals will begin to emerge, and actions will take shape as people consider the organization's role and its contributions to the future.

Consider the example of a college town that has a mission of providing high-quality public services while also being user-friendly and welcoming. By asking a small set of critical questions (below), leaders can help articulate goals that encourage specific strategies for doing just that.

1. *What new conditions would you like to see?*
    - *Example*: Newcomers have the information they need to successfully access town services.
2. *What changes would happen if these conditions were occurring?*
    - *Example*: Both newcomers and their neighbors are satisfied with the processes of moving and settling into their new homes and relationships.
3. *What important differences would you expect to see from these results?*
    - *Example*: People smoothly transition into their new lives in our town with little or no conflict between newcomers, old-timers, the town staff, and university partners.

By thoughtfully working through these critical questions, it is common for solutions to the problem to emerge.

- We could seek information from recent newcomers about what would have made their own move and integration more successful.
- We could create a website for newcomers with links to it from campus resources.
- We could designate one person, phone number, or place as the central contact for all newcomers. We could create more opportunities for town/gown interactions.

It is important for the group to avoid going to solutions right away—rather, the group's task is to capture the intent in a single goal statement: "Our goal as town government is to be welcoming and user-friendly for both new and existing residents in our town."

The conversation initially focuses on students coming to town to attend college, but the final goal benefits a wider group of newcomers. Conflicts between students and their neighbors might have been the catalyst for the discussion, but the goal addresses the more fundamental issue of customer service and welcoming people to the community. The "Drafting a Strategic Goal" activity will help your group draft goals.

Activity: Drafting a Strategic Goal

Strategic Goal: The Desired Situation

Clearly state the priority to be achieved: an attainable direction, change, or achievement. The desired change resulting from a focus on the priority.

To help stimulate your thinking, consider the following *before* you start writing your goals:

- To remain relevant, address emerging issues, overcome current challenges we need to . . .
- In order to successfully meet the needs, opportunities, and challenges of the next five years, we aspire to . . .

Sentence Structure and Key Terms

- Now describe the desired change you wish to see in broad terms to write your goal(s).

Example:

- *Newcomers will easily access the services and information they need to begin their new lives in our town.*

Phase Two—*Enact*: How Will We Get Where We Want to Go?

By the time the group completes the *envision* phase of the SPL cycle it will have generated many ideas that can be incorporated into specific and achievable objectives. Before the group moves to enact its vision, though, it needs to narrow and refine its focus and develop goals for a realistic handful of priorities. Toward that end, it is useful to reflect on the following questions:

- What kinds of changes do we want to see?
- What choices do we now need to make to help these changes take place?
- What actions do we now need to take to make these changes happen?

With a commitment to move ahead, the group is ready to enter the SPL cycle's second phase, *enact*, which also has two key processes—developing action plans and allocating resources to pursue them—each of which has products that will be included in the strategic plan (see Table 3).

Disciplined thinking is needed in moving through the *enact* phase. While broad stakeholders and key partners can help craft a compelling community vision, the effort to

Table 3. Key Processes, Activities, and Products in the SPL Cycle's *Enact* Phase

***Enact*: How Will We Get Where We Want to Go?**

Key Process	Activities	Products
Develop action plans	• Moving from goals to objectives • Assigning responsibilities	• SMART objectives • Action and responsibility plans
Allocate resources	• Budgeting for results	• Annual and long-term, capital budgets

narrow down to specific, measurable actions is best carried out by a more narrow group of decision-makers—typically members of a governing board and senior managers.

Key Process—Develop Action Plans: How Can We Make Each Goal Happen?

From the big buckets and strategic goals produced during the *envision* phase of the SPL cycle, participants should pull out the priorities that seem the most compelling—however that might be defined—and draft measurable objectives for pursuing them (see the activity "Developing SMART Objectives"). The key process in this part of the enacting phase is closely tied to work in areas such as performance management, performance measurement, and benchmarking in which organizations create systems for tracking key indicators and monitoring their progress.

As the group gets started, allow people to select goals that are most the compelling, urgent, and important to them and have them try to draft a measurable objective for each strategic goal. Make these statements available for others to read and consider. It is okay to let the draft objectives simmer among the decision-making group while staff members or a subcommittee works on refining the objective statements. During this process, more questions may emerge that the decision-making group will have to address. ("Do we want to focus solely on new college students arriving in our town, or do we broaden the scope to all residents needing service or information?") (See Figure 8.)

At a later date, review all of the proposed objectives and select the ones that are likely to have the most positive impact in helping the organization meet its desired goal. Chances are good that some participants will create a long list of detailed changes they want to see take place, but if the proposed changes are not strategic in nature, they belong in a work

Figure 8. Putting Goals into Action

- **What strategies will help us reach our objectives?**
- **Who will carry them out?**
- **Who will be responsible for what?**

Activity: Developing SMART Objectives

Sample Sentence Structure for Developing SMART Objectives

To [change]	[what]	By [#]	By [when]
• Increase • Decrease • Find a solution	• Might have to add "where" or "who" to be specific	• % change • # count • Might have to use best available proxy indicator	• Some future date

How to draft the sentence:

1. Identify the specific "what" you want to change.
2. Describe how you want to change it: Increase the "good" things that happen OR decrease the "bad" things that happen.
   - Try to express the change positively, if that is possible.
3. Establish a standard by which to measure and evaluate the amount of change.
4. Set a date by which the change will be evident.

plan, not in a goals and objectives document. For example, a strategic goal might be "to assure pedestrian safety and open access to all public buildings." This is a big goal that belongs in a strategic plan. However, "Fix the wobbly banister on the library steps" is a task that should go into an employee work plan. While fixing the banister is an activity that relates to the goal, it is not a "strategic goal." As mentioned above, the group needs to remain vigilant and discipline itself to focus on developing a few *strategic* objectives rather than listing numerous business-as-usual tasks.

The activity "Developing SMART Objectives" provides a standard sentence structure to use when writing objectives. The product produced from this activity is a set of SMART objectives, that is, objectives that are: Specific, Measurable, Aggressive (but Attainable), Results-oriented, and Time-bound. An example of a SMART objective might be, "By 2012, citizens will rate local streets 'acceptably clean' at least 90 percent of the time."

Often during the effort to draft SMART objectives, one or more people will say in response to a broadly stated goal, "We can't measure that!" Some things are indeed hard to measure directly. How, for instance, would you measure community pride or quality of life? In such cases, the group may agree to a set of proxy measures that will provide evidence relating to the goal. So, for example, the following proxy measures could be used in trying to gauge community pride:

- attendance at local sporting events,
- participation in community clubs and associations (Scouts, Rotarians, volunteer activities),
- attendance at community events (street fairs, concerts, food festivals),
- use of park and recreation facilities.

The following measures could be considered in trying to quantify a community's quality of life:

- high school graduation rates,
- trends in property values,
- homelessness statistics,
- obesity rates,
- use of food pantries and other social services.

To increase the likelihood that goals and objectives are accomplished, the organization needs a specific work plan that outlines "how" and "who" will be responsible for producing the indicators of progress or success. Responsibility for implementing the change will likely fall across multiple groups at all levels of the organization, starting with the governing board and management team and then moving down into multiple departments, units, and individuals within the organization. By sharing draft objectives with those who will be involved in carrying out the work, decision-makers get valuable input from the responsible groups and will describe more accurately how and when actions will occur and what results can be expected. In this process, people at multiple levels of the organization need to answer the questions, "What am I responsible for to make the vision a reality?" "What are others responsible for?" "How does our work fit together?"

Sequencing action plans appropriately so that they complement rather than compete with other expectations or developments can be critical. The working group, as well as the people who actually implement the change, benefit from clarity about the priority and timing of the work as well as the resources available to support it. If too many objectives are generated, or if the work falls to just one or two or a limited number of people, efforts are likely to falter. Make sure that the objectives are clearly tied to strategic goals and that responsibility for related actions is appropriately distributed; if too much work is piled on too few, the unexpected circumstances that inevitably arise will challenge your progress.

Activity: Getting Clear on the Desired Changes and How to Make Them Happen

How Will We Get There?

Discussion	Tasks
1. What broad conditions or results do we desire to see? 2. What would be happening if those results or conditions were occurring? 3. What important difference could we expect because of those changes? 4. What are we prepared to do first to help us reach our objectives?	*Decide on the priority goals* • Describe the results you seek to achieve. • Ensure that the goals are linked to the mission statement. • Set goals that should be achievable with effort. • Keep to a manageable number.
5. What do we intend to accomplish specifically? 6. What do we think will be different if we do this? 7. How will we know if we are successful? 8. When will we see results?	*Create SMART objectives that describe progress toward achieving the goals* • Give clear guidance about priority actions. • Draft objectives describing [what] will [change] by [how much #] and by [when]. • Circulate drafts to get input from those who are involved in the work.
9. Who will be responsible for doing what? 10. Have those responsible identified how they can be successful in carrying out this work?	*Develop action plans* • Assign responsibilities for making the objective happen. • Link action plans to performance expectations and resources.

Once SMART goals have been outlined in an action plan, leaders need to commit to follow through for successful implementation. Unless decision-makers provide support to those charged with implementing action plans, the priorities they have identified will be forgotten and the effort will have been wasted. To ensure that efforts to enact the strategic plan are carried out, governing boards and senior managers need to allocate sufficient resources for that effort.

Before allocating resources, though, first make sure that everyone is on the same page concerning what is to be done first, by whom, by when, and what measure will be used to monitor progress. Only after responsible parties and decision-makers agree on the work plan is it appropriate to move forward and allocate resources to support the planned work.

Key Process—Allocate Resources: What Is Needed to Achieve Our Goals?

As noted above, implementing the action plan will require decision-makers to allocate enough resources in terms of people, equipment, expertise, time, and financial support. Some of the necessary resources might either be in place or easily redirected toward a new focus. However, some goals may be different or big enough to require a major reorganization of current resources (such as redesigning the way groups work together in a new effort) or a major attempt to gain new resources (such as a bond referendum to fund construction).

Strategies are actions that require resources (see Figure 9). Resources are made available by the governing board and management through the annual budget process. The resources needed to support both short- and long-term strategies often flow upward from departmental plans and budgeting processes. Some local governments use a capital budgeting process to fund long-term strategies, often those requiring substantial investments over time, such as building new facilities and infrastructure.

Selecting funding strategies can be difficult even in good economic times. No organization gets to do all that it wants. Winnowing the list of funded priorities becomes especially difficult in bad economic times. Having agreed upon the vision, the mission, the values, and goals, leaders can use the SPL cycle to provide the context (and discipline) for strategy selection. The "Financial Reality Check" activity summarizes the questions and tasks in front of the decision-making group as they consider what their budget and fundraising options will enable them to do.

For complex, multifaceted goals (economic development), or for those that carry a very high price tag (repairing old or building new infrastructure), the first step is often to break the goal into manageable sub-goals that can be funded or financed over time. For large-scale capital projects the first step might be to explore how the work will be funded.

Figure 9. Strategies

- **Strategies are actions taken by an organization to make progress toward goals and objectives**
- **Funding strategies during the annual budget process represents the primary link between planning and budgeting**

Activity: Financial Reality Check

	Activities	Products
What Resources Do We Need?	• What goals will you fund, and why? • What level of funding are you prepared to commit to achieving your goals?	• Established and agreed upon criteria to use in making funding decisions • Budget documents linking priorities and goals to operating and capital budget allocations

Finding and securing financial support actually might be a more significant challenge than implementing the end goal.[5]

5. For more on local government budgeting see Julie M. Brenman with Gregory S. Allison, *Local Government Budgeting: A Guide for North Carolina Elected Officials*, UNC School of Government (SOG) Local Government Board Builders series (Chapel Hill: SOG, 2013).

Phase Three—*Evaluate*: Are We Making Progress? How Successful Are We?

For many organizations, strategic planning occurs when management and governing board leaders hold a retreat and agree on a handful of goals. Some will take this a step further and remember these goals as they propose budgets and allocate resources. Fewer have created systems to monitor, measure, and evaluate results. Too often strategic goals get lost as leaders respond to crises or get swept up by newer, shinier ideas begging for attention. There will always be opportunities to pursue new projects and services that would benefit communities. Some of these projects or issues may seem more interesting than monitoring and evaluating goals set months earlier during a planning retreat. If leaders stop paying attention to priorities others will too, and the strategic planning process will fail to achieve its intended goals.

Using the SPL planning cycle enables organizations and communities to *begin with the end in mind.* Taking time to measure, track, and assess progress provides leaders the opportunity to

- align daily actions with larger goals,
- provide information to the public about progress,
- demonstrate accountability and stewardship to the public,
- learn how to best strengthen the work moving forward,
- celebrate the outcomes of successful efforts toward shared goals.

In the third phase of the SPL cycle, leaders monitor progress and take time out to reflect on what has worked, what hasn't, and what can be improved. As with the previous phases in the SPL cycle, the evaluation phase has two key processes—monitoring and managing performance, and evaluating results—and these processes include activities and products that can be incorporated into the strategic planning portfolio. (See Table 4.)

Table 4. Key Processes, Activities, and Products in the SPL Cycle's *Evaluate* Phase

***Evaluate*—How Successful Are We?**

Key Processes	Activities	Products
Monitor and manage performance	• Milestones • Measures of success	• Annual calendar • Project reports
Evaluate results	• What did we do? • How well did we do? • How can we improve?	• Annual reports • Performance reviews • Gap analysis

Key Process—Monitoring and Managing Performance: How Are We Doing?

Different tools and methods are available for monitoring and managing performance. Working with employees from across the organization, senior managers should be responsible for identifying and implementing ways to effectively and efficiently collect information and report on progress made toward reaching the SMART objectives set in the *envision* phase. When an organization adopts and adheres to the SPL cycle, board members and employees alike can see how well their efforts are working and make needed adjustments to keep things on track.

The activity "Monitoring Progress" provides a framework for clarifying the who/what/when of tracking, assessing, or adjusting progress toward achieving goals and objectives. Making the effort early to clarify expectations can help avoid misunderstandings and build accountability into daily practice. It also provides a useful frame of reference in case of personnel transitions: institutional memory will not leave simply because a single person does.

Key Process—Evaluate Results: Are We There Yet?

Discipline is remembering what you want.—DAVID CAMPBELL[6]

By conducting a formal evaluation of the process and the people charged with carrying out the plan, the organization demonstrates its commitment to accountability and its record

6. See www.brainyquote.com/quotes/quotes/d/davidcampb172832.html.

Activity: Monitoring Progress

Are We Making Progress?

Activities	Products
• How will board priorities be aligned with management actions? • What information will be tracked? • How will information be reported and to whom? • How often will the governing board review progress? • How will adjustments be made?	• Listing of shared and individual responsibilities. • Identification of types of information to be tracked and who will collect it. • Calendar showing when periodic reporting will take place. • Assignments for reviewing and/or implementing changes to the plan.

for staying on track. Adjustments to any plan will, at times, be necessary. Unforeseen complications might arise. Unexpected opportunities might come up. Aspects of a new service or process might work beautifully in one neighborhood but not in another. To ensure that improvements occur continually and that learning is ongoing, evaluation should emphasize using an experience to enhance future performance rather than assigning blame when expectations are not fully met.

In response to the evaluation of what has been accomplished and what has not turned out as planned, people within the organization should be encouraged to find and propose new ways of aligning internal or external programs, strategies, and resources to accomplish the desired goals. The discussion during this process provides an opportunity to bring to the surface, and explore, a variety of possibilities for improving the plan and building capacity to accomplish the long-term vision.

Perhaps most important, this phase of the cycle provides the structure that enables the long-term sustainability of the work. The plan develops and adapts to new leaders and new opportunities while continuing to help the organization and community move toward a vision that current and future generations want to see.

An evaluation of the results is the only way to determine, to really know, if a plan is accomplishing what it was designed to achieve. The work of this key process focuses on collecting and reporting outcomes for the strategies set forth at the beginning of the year. Some results may seem small in comparison to the results for other strategic priorities. For instance, a project with the goal of building a new public facility may, by year's end, only have identified a way to fund the project, whereas another goal, the reduction of crime rates, may, as a result of smart policing and community engagement efforts, end up outpacing itself. Either way, the progress is real and the work helps move the community or organization toward its vision. It is therefore wise to use annual reports as a means of sharing both small and large achievements, keeping in mind that, by definition, strategic goals can take years to accomplish—if they were quick and easy to accomplish, they wouldn't be called *strategic*; they'd be called a to-do list.

Then, too, strategic goals cannot be accomplished by any one actor acting alone. Leaders need to make sure their strategic priorities align with employees' tasks and responsibilities, and employees need feedback to know if they are meeting expectations.[7] Integrating goals into job designs and performance reviews assures that employees understand their various roles in helping accomplish strategic goals. Governing boards too should reflect on how well their decisions and actions align with their goals and set priorities for their own work going forward.

A gap analysis simply shows what was expected at the outset of the planning process as compared with the actual result. The difference between the expected and the actual result is the *gap*. Sometimes the gap is small or nonexistent, in which case the goal is more likely to have been reasonable and realistic. In other cases, when gaps are large, a goal was perhaps too ambitious, was eclipsed by other work, or was too limited. Depending on the circumstances, leaders should reconsider and revise SMART objectives so that, moving forward, they better align with what can reasonably be accomplished in the next iteration of the SPL cycle (see Figure 10).

Activity: Evaluate Results

	Activities	Products
Are We There Yet?	1. What did we achieve? 2. How well did we do in accomplishing our goals? 3. How can we improve	• Annual reports • Performance reviews • Gap analysis

7. See Vaughn M. Upshaw, *How Are We Doing? Evaluating Manager and Board Performance*, UNC School of Government (SOG) Local Government Board Builders series (Chapel Hill: SOG, 2014).

Figure 10. Integrate and Align

Reality Checks: Tailoring the Process to Fit Your Needs

How Big Do We Want This Process to Be?

As alluded to in the first section (see "Why Plan?"), the process of planning cannot be designed until the organization's or the community's focus has been clearly defined. In general, the broader the scope of the planning process, the more stakeholders will be involved, the longer the process will take, and the more resources will be required to support the effort.

The focus can be relatively singular and/or simple, involving one organization, such as a municipal government. Alternatively, it can be broader and more complex, engaging every organization within a specific geographical area. The circumstances and issues of concern should define the scope of each party's involvement in defining a collective vision. The following questions can stimulate discussion on the scope of planning: What do we care about? Who else cares? Why do they care? How can we or others contribute to making positive change happen? Who or what could block our efforts?

The sidebar "Elements of Strategic Planning and Community Visioning" (pp. 10–11) outlines some potential differences to consider when deciding on the scope of the planning, whether at the board or organizational level or at the community level, for example. Whereas some issues will be specific to the organization itself—the goal of making an organization's services "user-friendly" would be one—other issues will necessitate multiple levels of involvement.

The broader the goal, though, the more complex and resource-intensive the effort becomes. When issues are complex or far-reaching (for example, closing the achievement gap or redesigning local economies), a broader approach is more likely to succeed, as no single organization has the power, resources, or authority necessary to tackle most social, environmental, or economic challenges.[8]

---

8. For additional information, see Reese and Berner, *Wicked Problems*.

How Much Citizen Engagement Is Enough?

Often, as a result of the enthusiasm elicited by starting a new planning effort, organizational leaders become highly optimistic about opportunities to seek and incorporate citizen input. Efforts like this are truly a great way of seeking out valuable perspectives and generating interest in community change.

The "Level of Involvement" sidebar (p. 8) presents a chart outlining the continuum of citizen involvement, from low to high. Each level of involvement is characterized by an interactive approach that seems justified and appropriate in particular situations. For instance, if the budget is restricted, the time frame is short, the enthusiasm is lacking, the opinions are uniformly held, or the leaders are strongly directive, *telling* citizens about the plan may be the default option. As resources become more expansive, though, and as leadership becomes more inclusive, perspectives become more diverse, or the passion becomes stronger, it makes sense to invest more time and energy in the process of exchanging information and asking for ideas from across the community. Again, the higher the citizen engagement, the longer and more resource-intensive the process will be. The important thing to remember is that behaviors need to match the language used to describe the process. If the leaders say, "We are creating this plan with and for you" but do not allow opportunities for input or co-creation of the plan, frustration and skepticism within the community are likely to result.

A high level of involvement, indicated by the *consulting* line of the chart, is easy and exciting to talk about but requires more time and resources than working on the *selling* or *telling* lines. To build trust within the community, public leaders should be transparent in describing how open or inclusive the planning process will be. There might be one particular decision—where to place a new elementary school, for example—that warrants more attention be paid to public hearings, focus groups, or stakeholder interviews.

Sometimes, citizen advisory committees (CACs) can be used to help the local government gather and filter information from the public. If the local government has CACs in place, these groups can be a good source of information about community priorities and interests. Creating a way for CACs to contribute to the development of strategic goals can help build commitment and support for programming and implementation efforts.[9]

Finally, consider pairing citizen engagement efforts with educational opportunities that help residents learn about the many programs and services offered by their local governments. Citizen education can demonstrate the breadth and value of what gets done

---

9. See Vaughn Mamlin Upshaw, *Creating and Maintaining Effective Local Government Citizen Advisory Committees*, with downloadable model policy and tracking forms, UNC School of Government (SOG) Local Government Board Builders series (Chapel Hill: SOG, 2010), https://www.sog.unc.edu/publications/books/creating-and-maintaining-effective-local-government-citizen-advisory-committees-downloadable-model.

by local government. Furthermore, educating citizens about particular topics—especially those that are often overlooked or have a technical tilt, such as, why water lines need to be repaired or replaced periodically or how the wastewater treatment plant functions—could elicit better informed suggestions.[10]

Are We Really Ready?

Like communication, accountability also works in more than one direction. Another important consideration for elected officials, in particular, is the extent to which they will be willing to support the process of developing and implementing the strategic plan. The SPL model holds both the staff and the governing board accountable for staying on track, practicing transparency, and engaging in mutual learning. Answers to the following questions might tease out the limits of organizational support:

- If the staff or community brings accurate data forward, will you give it careful and full consideration, even if it does not support your current views?
- If innovations designed to improve results are proposed, will you consider making changes to the status quo?
- If performance statistics show improved performance, will you congratulate those who made it happen?
- If performance declines, will you indicate concern but listen respectfully to explanations and plans for improvement?

Other groundwork requires an open discussion of the motivations to engage in an extensive strategic planning cycle and of the benefits that people hope to gain. The accompanying sidebar, "Background and Preparation," poses questions for discussion and enumerates some first steps to take.

---

10. See John B. Stephens, Ricardo S. Morse, and Kelley T. O'Brien, *Public Outreach and Participation*, UNC School of Government (SOG) Local Government Board Builders series (Chapel Hill, SOG: 2011), https://www.sog.unc.edu/publications/books/public-outreach-and-participation.

Background and Preparation

Are We Ready?

Discussion	Tasks
1. What prompts your organization or community to undertake this work? 2. What leads your organization or community to make the decision to proceed with one approach rather than another? Which circumstances help you make this decision? 3. How do you plan to move the work forward? 4. What added value do you perceive your organization or community will obtain by choosing this approach rather than another? 5. What challenges and opportunities will your intended approach present as you move forward? 6. Have we planned for the people, resources, and time required to do this well?	• Pick an approach. • Decide who will shepherd the process. • Decide how to involve others. • Confirm the time frame over which key events will take place. • Agree on the resources to be devoted to the process.

Appendix: The Basic Elements of a Strategic Plan

Strategic Goal: The desired situation

Objective: Conditions we want to create to move toward achieving the goal

Task: A method or approach taken to accomplish an objective

Actions: A set of related actions to carry out a set of tasks

Strategy: The total path or plan linking actions, tasks, objectives, and goals

What will it take to get there?

Additional information and guidance on strategic planning are available through the School of Government website, in particular, the Strategic Public Leadership microsite at https://www.sog.unc.edu/resources/microsites/strategic-public-leadership.